THE
MULLIGAN

A Parable of Second Chances

THE
MULLIGAN

Participant's Guide
Six Sessions

KEN BLANCHARD

— AND —

WALLY ARMSTRONG

WITH KEVIN HARNEY

ZONDERVAN.com/
AUTHORTRACKER
follow your favorite authors

ZONDERVAN

The Mulligan Participant's Guide
Copyright © 2010 by Wally Armstrong and Ken Blanchard

Requests for information should be addressed to:

Zondervan, *Grand Rapids, Michigan 49530*

ISBN 978-0-310-32896-4

Cover design: Rob Monacelli
Cover photography: Terzes Photography
Interior design: Matthew Van Zomeren

Printed in the United States of America

10 11 12 13 14 15 /DCI/ 23 22 21 20 19 18 17 16 15 14 13 12 11 10 9 8 7 6 5 4 3 2

CONTENTS

A WORD FROM KEN AND WALLY 7

SESSION ONE
PLAYING THE GAME OF LIFE FIRST . . .
DISCOVERING YOUR PURPOSE 11

SESSION TWO
THE ULTIMATE MULLIGAN . . .
THE BEST SECOND CHANCE EVER 21

SESSION THREE
THE COURSE LESS PLAYED . . .
LIVING WITH JESUS AS YOUR CADDY 31

SESSION FOUR
STARTING SLOWLY . . .
STRATEGIES FOR A GREAT LIFE 41

SESSION FIVE
UNLIMITED MULLIGANS . . .
EXPERIENCING TRUE FREEDOM 53

SESSION SIX
BECOMING AN OLD PRO . . .
INCREASING YOUR INFLUENCE 63

LEADER'S GUIDE: HOW TO LEAD A
SMALL GROUP DISCUSSION OF *THE MULLIGAN* 73

mulligan (*n*) — In friendly play, permission granted a golfer by the other players to retake a flubbed shot, especially the first shot of the game. Golf's generous forgiveness, The Mulligan, originated in the U.S. at Winged Foot Golf Club and was created by David B. Mulligan. This second-chance shot is not allowed by the official rules of golf.

A Word from Ken and Wally

When Wally Armstrong and I first met, we immediately became soul mates and friends because we shared two things in common. First, we both love golf and had played and enjoyed the game ever since we could walk. We never met a golf game we didn't like. To us, the worst a golf game can be is fabulous. Second, we both love Jesus—not as someone trapped in a church but as our friend and Savior who wants to walk with us both on the course and off.

The Mulligan brings these two loves together in a special way. My mission in life is to be a loving teacher and example of simple truths that help me and others awaken to the presence of God in our lives. I have a simple mind that can only comprehend simple truths. When I find such a truth, I want to tell other people about it. So when Wally first told me that Jesus is the greatest mulligan of all time, you could have knocked me over.

That was the most powerful, simple truth I had ever heard: we all need a few mulligans, not only on the golf course but in our lives. After all, none of us is perfect.

My mind started to soar with all kinds of thoughts about the power of a mulligan. First of all, it is not something you deserve or earn. Someone else has to give it to you. You can't just take a shot over in golf because you want to. The people playing with you have to say, "Why don't you take a mulligan?" Second, you have to be willing to receive it. Sometimes people's egos get in the way and they say, "Nah, forget it. I'll play it where it lies." Receiving a mulligan is not easy. And yet, if we're humble enough to accept it, we begin to realize our true potential.

My hope and prayer is that this study and the video teaching will help you discover, in new and fresh ways, that you have a friend in Jesus who is ready to forgive you and offer a mulligan every time you goof and make a bad shot. As this happens, you will learn to enjoy the game of life and golf more than you ever dreamed.

Ken Blanchard

As a young lad, my passion for golf grew out of the cornfields of Indiana. I hawked golf balls in the fields lining the local nine-hole Indian Lake Country Club. On a good day, my pockets were full of balls to be sold for a few nickels and dimes. But the real money came through caddying and shagging balls for the club champion Duke Dupree.

Duke saw my love and desire to play, so he taught me the disciplines of the game. More than that, he helped me believe in myself. He saw all the dormant possibilities in my life and made me believe they could come true. Duke was more than an employer. He was a teacher, brother, friend, and a father in many ways; Duke's impact on my life is immeasurable.

Deep relationships should stay with us throughout the course of our lives. I have been truly blessed with great friends; Ken Blanchard is one. When I met Ken a few years ago we connected instantly because we love the game and understand the great value of relationships. We believe that through relationships and second chances in life we have both gained a stronger grip on who we are and our ultimate purpose for living.

That is why our message is that life is a bowl full of mulligans — second chances abound!

Every one of us needs to take and learn from them. And, as we do, we will be strengthened to play the course laid out before us in golf and in life. It is my sincere desire and prayer that the message of this video curriculum, *The Mulligan*, will bring God's joy and hope your way.

Wally Armstrong

OF NOTE

The quotations interspersed throughout this participant's guide come from the book *The Mulligan* by Ken Blanchard and Wally Armstrong as well as from material gathered during the shooting of this video curriculum (Zondervan, 2010).

PLAYING THE GAME OF LIFE FIRST...

DISCOVERING YOUR PURPOSE

Life is an amazing gift and we enjoy every aspect of it more when we know our purpose and reason for living.

INTRODUCTION

Many of us spend our whole lives pursuing illusive things such as wealth, power, and status. These things are not bad, but if we make them the focal point of our existence, we will end up missing the greatest joys of life.

When we base our sense of value and worth on our performance and the opinions of others, we live on a perpetual roller coaster. If our performance is good and people affirm us, we feel great. But, if we are struggling to meet our goals and others begin to look down on us ... you know what happens. We begin to feel bad about who we are.

God wants to set us free from the ups and downs of a life based on how we perform. From the workplace, to our home, to the golf course, we don't have to live with the constant feeling that we must achieve at a certain level or else be a failure. When we have clarity about our life purpose and get first things first, our whole life makes sense, we live with lasting peace, and we actually have more fun in all we do!

The Bible clearly teaches that God establishes your significance and value. And, he says you are wonderful and worth more than you can imagine or dream. When you learn to see yourself through the loving eyes of God, you get a whole new perspective on life.

If you are looking for true significance and lasting joy, you must learn how to play the game of life first.

When we base our self-worth on our performance plus the opinion of others we will miss out on the joy of true significance.

Watch the session one video: ***Introduction, Golf Story, and Golf Tip***.

TALK ABOUT IT

Tell about a time on the golf course when you got a mulligan (a second chance) and how this impacted your game and attitude.

Ken says, "Significance is really about generosity of time, talent, treasure, and touch." Tell about a person you know who has lived a significant life filled with generosity. How has that person impacted the lives of others?

> You become an adult when you realize you are here to serve
> and not to be served, to give and not to get.

*Watch the session one video: **Main Session with Wally and Closing Challenge with Ken**. Use the Video Teaching Notes section on the next page to record your thoughts and reflections.*

VIDEO TEACHING NOTES

Our purpose in this life (Psalm 139)

God delights in you ... even when you mess up (Psalm 37)

A "human being" or a "human doing"

What drives us?

What is your number-one priority?

What will help us discover God's purpose and love?

Closing reflections with Ken

VIDEO DISCUSSION

Explore as many of the following questions as your group has time for.

1. **Read:** Psalm 139:1–14, 23–24. What do you learn about yourself as you read this psalm?

   What do you learn about God from this psalm?

   What do you learn about how God sees you and interacts with you?

2. **Read:** Psalm 37:3–7, 23–24. In this psalm, God calls us to do a number of things. What are these things, and how can they help you live a life of significance?

3. Wally says that the Bible just assumes that we will stumble, fall, and mess up at times. How do you feel when you realize that God knows you will make mistakes and that he still loves you?

What keeps you from experiencing the love of God during those times when you have recently stumbled and fallen?

4. Wally talks about the drive when he was younger to achieve and perform so that he would feel valued and significant. This drive can turn us into a "human doing" and keep us from experiencing true joy. What are some signs that we are becoming a "human doing" rather than a "human being"?

5. Tell about a time in your life when you realized that God loves you and values you even though you mess up and make mistakes. How did this impact your relationship with God?

6. Both Ken and Wally talk about how we often find our significance in our performance and the opinions of others. Why is this, and how can we overcome this temptation to base our self-worth on something so precarious?

7. In the book, *The Mulligan*, there is a moment when the main character gets so mad that he snaps his putter over his knee during a Pro-Am golf event because he leaves a critical putt just short. Tell about a time when you "lost it" and how God's grace helped you through that situation.

8. Wally says that some people compartmentalize their lives like a TV dinner. God gets one little section but not the whole thing. What are some of the ways we compartmentalize life and God?

Instead of a TV dinner, Wally says our lives should be like a chicken pot pie, and God is like the gravy ... flowing through every part of life and every activity we engage in. What can we do to let God move through every part of our lives?

Significance is really about generosity of time,
talent, treasure, and touch.

Closing Prayer

Take time as a group to pray in some of the following directions:

- Praise God that you are "wonderfully made" (Psalm 139). Ask him to help you base your self-worth on how he sees you, not on how you perform or the opinions of other people.
- Thank God for loving you just as you are but also for loving you enough to help you become more than who you are today.
- Pray for the other members of your group to open their hearts to hear the message of the mulligan (God's grace). Pray that this study will have a powerful impact on all of your lives.

BETWEEN SESSIONS

Personal Reflection

Take time in the coming week to notice what impacts your moods and responses. Are you happy only when you perform well and others take note of your accomplishments? Do you get down or frustrated when things don't go just right? Do you walk through your day with a confidence that God loves you and you are valuable simply because God says so?

Personal Action

Use the journal space at the end of this session and try the experiment Paul used in *The Mulligan*. Reflect on the past day or two and write down some of your "good shots" in the game of life. What did you do well? When did you have a great attitude? Who did you care for? Then, write down a few areas you need a mulligan. What would you like to do over and how will you change things next time? If you run out of space, get a journal or notebook and keep writing.

Recommended Reading

As you reflect on what you have learned in this session, read chapters 1–6 of *The Mulligan* by Ken Blanchard and Wally Armstrong.

In preparation for the next session, read chapters 7–13 of *The Mulligan*.

JOURNAL

Solid Shots

_____

_____

_____

_____

_____

_____

_____

Mulligans

_____

_____

_____

_____

_____

_____

_____

SESSION 2

THE ULTIMATE MULLIGAN ...
THE BEST SECOND CHANCE EVER

The Ultimate Mulligan is the amazing offer that God extends to everyone in the world. It is the invitation to have a relationship with him through faith in Jesus Christ.

INTRODUCTION

We all love gifts. Children go to bed on Christmas Eve trembling with excitement and have a hard time going to sleep. Their anticipation of the presents awaiting them fills their young minds. Even as adults, we become like little kids again when someone offers us a gift. We get excited!

The Ultimate Mulligan is the greatest gift in all of human history. Just like a mulligan in golf, it has to be offered ... and it has been. God entered our world on the first Christmas. Jesus was a gift like no other. He was God wrapped in human flesh. Jesus came to live a sinless life, died on a cross in our place to pay for our sins, and rose again after three days and won the victory over sin and death. Jesus is the best mulligan ever.

On the golf course a mulligan gets us a fresh ball on the tee and saves us a shot or two on our scorecard. The Ultimate Mulligan of Jesus gives us a new start in life, forgiveness from every wrong thing we have ever done, a friendship with God, and the hope of heaven. Now that's a second chance like no other.

The Ultimate Mulligan is not a *what*, but a *who*.

Watch the session two video: **Introduction, Golf Story, and Golf Tip**.

TALK ABOUT IT

Wally tells a story about a strange thing that happened to him on a tough par four during a PGA tournament. Tell about something odd or surprising that has happened to you on a golf course.

God is only one conversation away.

Watch the session two video: **Main Session with Wally and Closing Challenge with Ken**. *Use the Video Teaching Notes section on the next page to record your thoughts and reflections.*

VIDEO TEACHING NOTES

What is the Ultimate Mulligan?

A journey to Jesus

What is the ultimate conversation?

Would God offer a mulligan to me?

How do I get the Ultimate Mulligan?

Closing reflections with Ken

VIDEO DISCUSSION

Explore as many of the following questions as your group has time for.

1. In the session introduction Ken talks about the difference between religion and following Jesus. Religion is spelled "D-O," and it is all about how we act, behave, and perform. But following Jesus is spelled "D-O-N-E," and it is about what God has done for us through Christ. How can this simple definition give us a true picture of the Christian faith?

2. You can't just *take* a mulligan in the game of golf. Someone has to *offer* it to you. The Ultimate Mulligan is a gift offered by God. What has God done to make this gift available to you?

   If you have received the gift of the Ultimate Mulligan, tell your story about when you first opened your heart to believe in Jesus Christ.

3. **Read:** John 3:16 and Ephesians 2:8–9. What is the source of the Ultimate Mulligan, and what do we need to do to receive this amazing gift?

4. Wally talks about how (as a college student) he believed that being a follower of Jesus was all about rules and regulations ... things he had to do and stop doing. How does this kind of thinking keep people from entering a relationship with Jesus? When we understand that our works are not the key to salvation and a relationship with Jesus, how can this reality set us free?

5. Some people feel that they don't deserve God's ultimate gift of forgiveness. What makes people feel this way, and what would you say to a friend who declared, "I just don't know if God could forgive someone like me?"

6. If you have had a chance to see a friend, family member, or acquaintance receive Jesus and accept the Ultimate Mulligan, tell about this experience. How did this person's life change after accepting this amazing gift?

7. Ken wraps up the session by talking about how God makes up the difference for us (from 1 – 100). We are not perfect—but Jesus, through his life and sacrifice, provides all that we lack. How might this simple idea help you communicate the message of the Ultimate Mulligan to a person in your life who has not yet embraced the grace of Jesus?

8. Ken tells about how God used Bob Buford to help him understand the message of God's grace and take a step toward faith in Jesus. Name one person God used to help you accept the Ultimate Mulligan. What was it about that person's life, attitude, or words that connected with you on your spiritual journey?

> We stand tallest before God when we are on our knees.

CLOSING PRAYER

Take time as a group to pray in some of the following directions:

- Thank God that the best mulligan in the entire world is as close as a prayer for all who will accept Jesus.
- Thank God for the people he placed in your life who shared their faith, prayed for you, and helped you meet Jesus.
- Ask God to use you to naturally communicate his love and grace (the message of the Ultimate Mulligan) to the people in your life who still need to meet Jesus. Ask him to prepare their hearts for the new life that Jesus offers.

BETWEEN SESSIONS

Personal Reflection

Consider the people God has placed in your life who have not yet received Jesus, the Ultimate Mulligan: family members, friends, neighbors, work colleagues. How can you pray more intentionally for these people? What opportunities might you have to tell them your story of coming to faith in Jesus? How can you serve and love one of these people in a way that would shine the light and love of Jesus?

Personal Action

Make a list of three or four people who were instrumental in your journey toward faith in Jesus. Call these people in the coming days and thank them for their witness, prayers, and gentle diligence as an influencer in your life. If they have been an "old pro" to you, give them *The Mulligan* and tell them that God used them in your life just as he used the old pro in the story of *The Mulligan*.

Continue developing a pattern of writing in your journal a few times each week.

Recommended Reading

As you reflect on what you have learned in this session, read chapters 7 – 13 of *The Mulligan* by Ken Blanchard and Wally Armstrong, if you haven't already done so.

In preparation for the next session, read chapters 14 and 15 of *The Mulligan*.

Journal

Solid Shots

_____

_____

_____

_____

_____

_____

_____

Mulligans

_____

_____

_____

_____

_____

_____

_____

THE COURSE LESS PLAYED ...

LIVING WITH JESUS AS YOUR CADDY

We can't make it through life on our own. We all need someone to walk at our side and help us along the way. Jesus wants to be so close to us that we can feel him near us each moment of every day.

INTRODUCTION

For many, many years golf was a team game. A golfer and a caddy would walk together, talk, and make decisions in partnership. The pros still have this close-knit relationship with a caddy. But many amateurs have never experienced the help and support that comes with talking through each shot with someone who has studied and knows the course.

Jesus wants to be your caddy.

He knows his Father's course better than we ever could. He is ready to tell us about hidden hazards, subtle breaks in the green—and he can line us up on every shot. What we need to do is ask for his wisdom, listen for his counsel, and trust that he knows what he is talking about.

When we do, the course less played gets a lot easier. We spend less time in life's bunkers and hazards. We are more prone to stay in bounds. Jesus wants to be more than simply the Savior who washes away your sins. He wants to be a friend and companion who guides you every step of the way. He wants to be your caddy.

Watch the session three video: **Introduction, Golf Story, and Golf Tip**.

TALK ABOUT IT

Ken tells about getting a phone call and learning that his home had burned to the ground. At that moment he was faced with the reality that in the midst of great loss and real pain, he was not alone. In the middle of a brutally painful time, peace and joy invaded his life. Describe a time when you faced something very difficult and God showed up, bringing peace and joy to your heart.

Christ died for me ... the least I can do is live for him.

*Watch the session three video: **Main Session with Wally and Closing Challenge with Ken**. Use the Video Teaching Notes section on the next page to record your thoughts and reflections.*

VIDEO TEACHING NOTES

Finding God's plan and design for your life

Some wrong thinking that can creep into our minds and hearts

The most important "second conversation"

Becoming a friend and companion of Christ

How can I shift from performance to a friendship with Jesus?

What matters most to God? Receiving his love

Closing reflections with Ken

Trust your caddy, Jesus. Always remember, he is your friend and wants to walk with you as you play his Father's course. He is ready to help you avoid focusing on obstacles and trouble spots so you can play the kind of game you were meant to play.

The Old Pro

VIDEO DISCUSSION

Explore as many of the following questions as your group has time for.

1. Wally talks about how he became a workhorse for God after accepting Jesus and how his acts of service were driven by a deep feeling that he still needed to perform to get God's love. How can this kind of feeling creep into our hearts, and what can we do to really see and embrace God's amazing love?

2. **Read:** John 15:12–15. What does Jesus teach us about himself in this passage? And what does he teach about how he sees us?

3. The most important conversation we can ever have is when we accept Jesus and his Ultimate Mulligan. But there is a critically important second conversation. This is when we learn to talk with Jesus, like a friend, as we walk through our daily life. Tell about a way you have learned to connect with Jesus in a natural and conversational way ... like a personal friend.

4. If you experienced a change in your relationship with Jesus—from performing or trying to please him to becoming his friend—share what helped you make this shift. How has this affected your Christian faith?

5. **Read:** Hebrews 12:1–3. How does keeping our eyes on Jesus and knowing him as a friend help us live for him and know the right path to take?

6. Wally really believes that having a friendship with Jesus and walking with him as a daily companion will strengthen our faith and help us say no to temptations and yes to obedience. How might your life change if you went through your normal day aware of the fact that Jesus is right there, walking by your side?

7. **Read:** Matthew 22:37–40. Respond to this statement: "We can't really love others until we love ourselves. When we see ourselves the way God sees us and learn to love ourselves, we will be empowered to extend God's love more freely to others."

8. Ken wraps up this session sharing how he walks with Jesus as his caddy on a daily basis. Ken actually talks with Jesus and says things like, "Jesus, what do you think I should do here?" or "Jesus, feel free to interrupt me here because you know what needs to be said." What are some questions you might begin asking Jesus through the day, and how might he whisper answers to you?

9. If you have experienced Jesus whispering in your ear, like a caddy giving you help and direction, what did he say and how did it give direction to your life?

God is a whole lot more concerned with who we are
than what we are doing!

CLOSING PRAYER

Take time as a group to pray in some of the following directions:

- Thank Jesus for being so interested in your life that he wants to walk with you, side by side, through each day.
- Pray for wisdom to ask Jesus good questions and for patience to listen quietly for his whispered answers and directions.
- Praise God for the many hazards and bunkers you have avoided through the years because Jesus has directed your steps ... thank him for the dangers and obstacles he protected you from that you didn't even know about or notice.

Between Sessions

Personal Reflection

Think about your relationship with Jesus. Is it really a friendship? Do I talk with him and expect him to actually respond? Do I listen for his voice? **Read:** John 10:2–15. If I am a sheep and Jesus is my Shepherd, what does this passage say about my capacity to hear and recognize his voice?

Personal Action

Make time each day, for the coming week, to be quiet and listen to God. Make your own list of questions, or use some of the ones provided below. Simply ask a question and then take a minute or two and be quiet as you listen for the voice of your Caddy.

- What have you done to show me your love and grace?
- Is there someone in my life who needs a word of encouragement? If so, what should I say to this person?
- Is there a pattern or behavior in my life that I should stop?
- Is there something new in my life I should begin?
- Is there someone who needs an act of kindness or service and how might you use me to care for this person?
- As I go into a new day, is there something you want me to add to my schedule?
- Add your own questions . . .

Continue developing a pattern of writing in your journal a few times each week. Take some time to review the past couple weeks in your journal and see where you are growing.

Recommended Reading

As you reflect on what you have learned in this session, read chapters 14 and 15 of *The Mulligan* by Ken Blanchard and Wally Armstrong, if you haven't already done so.

In preparation for the next session, read chapter 10 of *The Mulligan*.

What Jesus wants from you is your attention and your friendship. A friendship with Jesus will transform your life and turn it into an adventure.

JOURNAL

Solid Shots

_____

_____

_____

_____

_____

_____

_____

Mulligans

_____

_____

_____

_____

_____

_____

_____

Session 4

Starting Slowly ...
Strategies for a Great Life

Most of us tend to launch out of bed with a driven attitude. We can set the pace for a better day when we start slowly and make space to connect with God.

INTRODUCTION

The alarm clock breaks the silence of the night and we shoot out of bed like a horse out of the gate at the Kentucky Derby. "And they're off!"

If we are not careful, we can let our external and task-oriented self push us so hard that we collapse in bed at night and don't even notice that we never slowed down, reflected, enjoyed God's presence, connected with the people around us, or truly experienced our day.

Just as getting to the golf course a little early and spending a few moments stretching leads to a better and more satisfying round of golf, entering our day slowly makes for a better life. Jesus actually had strategies for keeping his focus on the most important things—and we can learn from his example.

As we make a decision to dial back our driven nature and connect with God in meaningful ways, we end up being more productive, more joyful, and more fulfilled.

> The problem with a rat race is that even if
> you win it, you're still a rat.
>
> *Lily Tomlin*

Watch the session four video: **Introduction, Golf Story, and Golf Tip.**

TALK ABOUT IT

Ken suggests that we all have two distinct selves: an external, task-oriented self that is all about getting jobs done *and* a thoughtful, reflective self. Which of these parts of you wakes up first in the morning and naturally moves you into your day?

How is your day impacted if your external, task-oriented self runs your day and your thoughtful, reflective self never wakes up?

Make life a special occasion and not a speed bump as you race through your day.

*Watch the session four video: **Main Session with Wally and Closing Challenge with Ken**. Use the Video Teaching Notes section on the next page to record your thoughts and reflections.*

VIDEO TEACHING NOTES

We can tend to rush into our day if we are not careful

The Chair ... discovering the transforming friendship of Jesus

Why is it important to walk with Jesus all the time?

What will help me start my day slowly?

Closing reflections with Ken

VIDEO DISCUSSION

Explore as many of the following questions as your group has time for.

1. Ken points out that Jesus had four strategies for living that we can all learn from:

   • Solitude (time to be alone and quiet)
   • Prayer (time to talk with the Father)
   • Study of Scripture (time to reflect on truth)
   • Being part of a small group (time to connect in a consistent and meaningful way with people)

   How might each of these help you live a life of meaning and significance?

2. Starting our day slowly can help set the tone for all we will experience and even for how we respond to people and surprises along the way. If you have tried to develop a strategy for starting your day slowly and really connecting with God, how have you seen this practice impact your day?

   What are some of the things you have done to help you start slowly and get your mind and heart calibrated for the day?

3. **Read:** 2 Timothy 4:6–8. In this passage we see the apostle Paul reflecting back on his life. What does he say about himself (and his life), and how might these ideas inspire you in your desire to walk with Jesus each and every day?

4. Some people talk about Jesus as if he is an actual friend they walk with and talk with through their day. Wally talks about having a "transforming friendship" with Jesus. What habits have you discovered that help you grow a friendship with Jesus?

   What gets in the way of this kind of intimacy in your relationship with the Savior?

5. If we are intentional about starting our day with Jesus, we can also invite him to come along with us for the rest of the day. When you think through your normal week, what are some of the places you go where you would naturally want to invite Jesus to come with you, and how might an awareness of his presence transform who you are in those places?

6. What are some of the places we might be reluctant to invite Jesus to walk side by side with us? How might an awareness that Jesus is with us impact our decisions as we enter these places, or decide not to enter these places?

7. Wally talks about how most golfers like to practice with the driver. But about 60 percent of our shots are wedges and putts, and we tend to avoid practicing these little shots that really make a difference in our score. The same is true in life. It is the little things that seem to make the biggest difference. Tell about a time you learned to trust God in what seemed to be a small area of life and how it made a bigger impact than you thought.

8. The theme of journaling has come up a number of times through this study. If you have been trying to journal, how has this gone for you? What has made it tough? What has been valuable? If journaling has helped you connect with God and express your heart to him in new ways, what advice would you give to someone who has not yet tried journaling?

9. Ken talks about doing three things each morning to help set the direction and tone for his day:

- Reading his **mission statement**: "To be a loving teacher and example of simple truths that helps myself and others to awaken to the presence of God in our lives."
- Looking at his own **obituary** (he's written one in advance!)
- Reviewing his **four driving values**: spiritual peace, integrity, love, and joy

How might adding this simple strategy to the start of your day help you live a more fruitful and focused life?

God has given us an imagination and we can use it for him. Sometimes, we have to start by imagining Jesus is with us, and with time, our imagination grows up into faith.

CLOSING PRAYER

Take time as a group to pray in some of the following directions:

- Thank God that he is personal and wants to start the day with you, walk with you through all you experience, and finish by your side. Praise him for being that interested and personal.
- Ask God to help you determine the right things to start your day slowly and really connect you to him.
- Surrender to God all the things that seem to drive you and push you to rush past what matters most in life.

Between Sessions

Personal Reflection

Ken can quote his personal mission statement from memory because it is short and clear: *"To be a loving teacher and example of simple truths that helps myself and others to awaken to the presence of God in our lives."* Each morning he reviews this statement and lets it help him prepare for the day.

In the coming days reflect on what you believe your personal mission in life should be. You might even want to use the space provided below to write a draft or two of your personal mission statement. If you do, begin reviewing it in the morning as you rise and see how this simple process of focusing on what matters most helps set the tone and direction for your day.

My Mission Statement (Draft #1)

My Mission Statement (Draft #2)

My Mission Statement (Draft #3)

Personal Action

Try the "Chair" challenge. One or two mornings in the coming week, sit somewhere quiet and place a chair near you. As you read the Bible, pray, experience silence, and seek to start your day slowly, imagine Jesus sitting there with you (because he really is there). Talk to him (aloud or silently) about what you read in the Bible and have a conversation with him (because that's what prayer really is).

Write your own obituary. Include those things you would love to have someone write about you at the end of your life. Then, tuck this in your Bible and look at it on a regular basis. You might even want to make this one of your starting-slow strategies. Ask yourself and God how you can live each day in a way that will help you become the person he wants you to be.

Continue developing a pattern of writing in your journal a few times each week. Be sure to celebrate the good shots!

Recommended Reading

As you reflect on what you have learned in this session, read chapter 10 of *The Mulligan* by Ken Blanchard and Wally Armstrong, if you haven't already done so.

In preparation for the next session, read chapter 12 of *The Mulligan*.

> As time passes, the more I walk with Jesus, I see myself as a "We," and not so much as a "Me."

JOURNAL

Solid Shots

_____

_____

_____

_____

_____

_____

_____

Mulligans

_____

_____

_____

_____

_____

_____

_____

SESSION 5

UNLIMITED MULLIGANS ...

EXPERIENCING TRUE FREEDOM

God offers unlimited grace and forgiveness. When we know that God will always forgive us, we discover a new desire to do the right things and live in ways that honor Jesus. Knowing we have unlimited mulligans does not cause us to play worse, but they free us to play the game of life with increased freedom and confidence.

INTRODUCTION

It is the craziest thing. It just seems that any time a golfer hits a poor shot and then drops another ball to try again, the second shot is so much better!

Why is that?

It is because the second shot does not count, the pressure is off, and we relax.

Have you ever heard someone say, "If I could just play a second shot every time, I could make it on the PGA tour!"? What they are really saying is, "If I could just relax and hit the best shot that is in me on the first try, I could play amazing golf." And they are right.

This simple illustration from golf carries right over to our life and friendship with Jesus. When we get the truth of God's amazing grace and his promise of never-ending forgiveness (mulligans) ... we just play better. We know we are loved and it sets us free. We are not trying to impress or please some angry heavenly Parent. When we discover that we are precious to God, loved, forgiven — and his grace is never-ending — we are freed to respond to him as trusting children.

> When I know I have a second chance, I do not put the same pressure on myself and I just seem to play better.

Watch the session five video: **Introduction, Golf Story, and Golf Tip**.

TALK ABOUT IT

Why is it that when a golfer gets a second shot—a mulligan—it seems like they always do better?

Ken is confident that knowing the constant forgiveness of Jesus will actually empower us to avoid doing wrong things and make more choices that bring joy to God and to us. In other words, knowing you can have a spiritual mulligan will lead to freedom that allows you to play the game of life better. How do you respond to this idea?

Forgiveness is love in action.

*Watch the session five video: **Main Session with Wally and Closing Challenge with Ken**. Use the Video Teaching Notes section on the next page to record your thoughts and reflections.*

VIDEO TEACHING NOTES

No more condemnation

Don't run *from* God, run *to* God

Does God ever run out of forgiveness?

What can I do when I am not feeling God's forgiveness?

Closing reflections with Ken

VIDEO DISCUSSION

Explore as many of the following questions as your group has time for.

1. During his golf story, Wally talks about how Lee Trevino told him to forget the shot he missed before and look forward to the next one. In Philippians 3:13–14 the apostle Paul writes, "But one thing I do: Forgetting what is behind and straining toward what is ahead, I press on toward the goal...." Why is it important to let the past go and look forward to what lies ahead, in both golf and life?

2. **Read:** Romans 7:15–20 and 8:1–4. Describe a time you felt like Paul feels in Romans 7:15–20.

   According to Romans 8:1–4, what has God done to remove the judgment and condemnation that comes because of sin (all the wrongs we have done)? How can knowing this forgiveness and being confident in it lead to freedom in your daily life?

3. Wally tells a story about two kids: one ran from Mom when he was in trouble and the other ran right to her. What are some of the ways we run from God and avoid him (and his people) when we have made mistakes and are struggling with sin?

4. The best place to run when we are in midst of battling sin or temptation is straight to God. Tell about a time you were struggling in some area of your life but went to God and told him all about it. How did this impact your relationship?

5. Wally talks about the very real struggle many of us have actually receiving God's love and grace on a daily basis. What are some of the things that get in the way of us embracing God's love and really accepting it? What has helped you get over the feeling that you don't deserve the love and grace of Jesus?

6. **Read:** Romans 8:31 – 39. These are some of the most uplifting and hope-filled words in the Bible. As a group, list all the things God promises and says about followers of Jesus in this passage.

What new freedom and confidence might come into your life if you lived every day aware that this is how God sees you?

7. Ken talks about how living with confidence in God's unending mulligans helps us learn from our mistakes rather than repeat them over and over again. Tell about a time that God used a poor choice or wrong action in your life to teach you a lesson that has made you a better person and a more faithful follower of Jesus.

8. Sometimes God offers us a mulligan — and we accept — but some people still want to heap condemnation on us. What can help us keep our focus on the grace of God and not the criticism and judgmental attitudes of such individuals?

9. **Read:** Matthew 6:9–15. What can we do to increase our capacity to forgive those who have wronged us?

Why is it so important that we extend grace and forgiveness in the way God has offered it to us?

> The more I become aware that I have unlimited mulligans,
> the fewer mulligans I seem to need.

CLOSING PRAYER

Take time as a group to pray in some of the following directions:

- Thank God that his grace never ends and that you can always have one more mulligan.
- Ask God to spare you from taking advantage of his grace. Pray that the confidence you have in his forgiveness will lead you to new levels of freedom to be obedient to his will and plan for your life.
- Praise God that his grace is so big that you can share it freely with others and never run out.
- Confess that you can be tempted to receive God's grace but forget to extend it to others.

Between Sessions

Personal Reflection

Make a commitment to be extravagant with mulligans in the coming week. Pray for eyes to see where people need a word of grace and a second chance. Look for opportunities and situations where God's grace-filled mulligans are not offered freely and do what you can to bring an overflow of grace into this setting.

Personal Action

One of the best gifts we can give to another person is a living example of unlimited mulligans. Just as we have been forgiven and receive God's grace every single day, we are invited to extend that same kind of forgiving attitude toward others. If there is a person in your life who has wronged you, but you are still holding it against them, talk to God about this. You might want to read the parable in Matthew 18:21–34 that addresses this exact issue. Then, pray for a heart that forgives just as Jesus forgives and take actions that will extend grace to this person who has wronged you.

Continue developing a pattern of writing in your journal a few times each week. Be honest about where you need mulligans and trust that God offers them freely.

Recommended Reading

As you reflect on what you have learned in this session, read chapter 12 of *The Mulligan* by Ken Blanchard and Wally Armstrong, if you haven't done so already.

In preparation for the next session, read chapters 14–18 of *The Mulligan*.

The biggest thing I learned from having unlimited mulligans is to not beat myself up for my mistakes, but to learn from them.

JOURNAL

Solid Shots

_____

_____

_____

_____

_____

_____

_____

Mulligans

_____

_____

_____

_____

_____

_____

_____

SESSION 6

BECOMING AN OLD PRO ...
INCREASING YOUR INFLUENCE

God's plan for you impacts more than just your life. God wants to increase your influence and bring the message of his mulligan through you to others.

INTRODUCTION

In the story of the mulligan, the businessman, Paul, encounters Will Dunn, the Old Pro! When he does, his life is never the same.

The Old Pro has a deep, authentic, and living friendship with Jesus, his caddy. The way Will Dunn walks with Paul is an example to us all. At the end of the book we discover that the Old Pro is investing his life in far more people than just Paul. He spends time with adults and kids, with golfers and people he meets on his morning walks, and with those who can pay for a round of golf and those who can't afford a lunch.

It seems that Old Will Dunn has discovered the joy of loving people and sharing the simple story of God's Son, Jesus, the Ultimate Mulligan. As we read *The Mulligan* it becomes clear that influencing others with the message of Jesus is not primarily about memorized tactics and special projects. It is really a natural and organic part of daily life.

The truth is, every follower of Jesus can be an Old Pro to someone. There are people we know who need to discover the joy and freedom that comes with receiving the Ultimate Mulligan and living with Jesus as their caddy.

God uses ordinary people who have extraordinary
love for others.

Watch the session six video: **Introduction, Golf Story, and Golf Tip**.

TALK ABOUT IT

Tell about someone who has been a mentor, coach, or Old Pro in your life. How has that person's life influenced you?

Being an Old Pro is not about age; it is about
the condition of our heart.

Watch the session six video: **Main Session with Wally and Closing Challenge with Ken.** *Use the Video Teaching Notes section on the next page to record your thoughts and reflections.*

VIDEO TEACHING NOTES

Why Jesus came to this earth and why we are here

Focus on what matters most

The Great Commandment

The three Es
     Engage

     Enjoy

     Encourage

Why is it so important to forgive ourselves?

Could I become an old pro?

Closing reflections with Ken

Wrap-up with Wally

> The more we become an old pro to others, the more God
> will draw old pros to be part of our life.

VIDEO DISCUSSION

Explore as many of the following questions as your group has time for.

1. In the session introduction Ken talked about how an authentic life of faith will cause people to ask us why we are so forgiving, caring, kind, and loving. Name one person who modeled a dynamic Christian life for you. How did that person's example impact your desire to know Jesus?

   Tell about a time when someone asked you about why you are different in the way you love, serve, or care. How did that question open the door for you to share your faith in Jesus?

2. Wally talks about the need for us to be careful that we don't get caught up in the things we will leave behind. Instead, we need to focus on that which will last forever—and relationships are at the top of the list! What are some of the temporary things that can seem very important but distract us from what is most important?

   What can we do to stay focused on the things that matter most and avoid investing too much time on the things we will leave behind when this life is over?

3. Who are some of the people you love and care about that have not yet experienced the joy of the Ultimate Mulligan that is found in Jesus? How can your group members pray for you as you try to share the message of God's love with these people?

4. **Read:** Matthew 28:16–20 and Acts 1:7–8. What does Jesus say about our part in helping others learn about the Ultimate Mulligan, living with Jesus as your caddy, unlimited mulligans, and all the good news you have learned in this small group study?

5. Wally suggests three Es that will help us become old pros at learning to share God's love with others. What are practical ways we can do each of these?

   • Engage

   • Enjoy

   • Encourage

6. In the book, *The Mulligan*, the Old Pro is really an example of a disciple. What were some of the ways he walked with his friend Paul and showed patience, grace, love, and other qualities we all want to have in our lives?

How could you take some of what you learned from the example of the Old Pro and weave it into your daily life?

7. Ken shares about how he had family members who were old pros and big influencers in his life. Who is one person in your family that God might want you to be an old pro to? What is the next step you can take toward strengthening this relationship and influencing the life of this person?

8. What was one big lesson you learned from *The Mulligan* study, and how will this impact your life?

CLOSING PRAYER

Take time as a group to pray in some of the following directions:

- Thank God for the old pros he has placed in your life.
- Ask God to help you take seriously the opportunity you have to influence others and be an old pro to them.
- Praise God that he has not sent us into the journey of life alone, but that he walks with us and brings people to walk by our side.
- Pray for strength to instill the lessons from *The Mulligan* into your daily life.

IN THE COMING DAYS

Personal Reflection

At the end of *The Mulligan*, Paul meets a young man named Tim who is sitting on the porch of the municipal golf course where he had met with the Old Pro on so many occasions. Although Paul did not really see himself as old pro material, God opened the door for a new relationship and Paul walked through it. Keep your eyes open in the coming weeks. There are people all around you who need someone to model and share the love of Jesus. Be open to God's leading and prompting.

Personal Action

Get on the phone, write a note, or drop by the house of someone who has been an old pro in your life. Take time to let them know how much they mean to you and thank them for sharing the best news ever with you.

If a person who has been an old pro in your life has passed away and is already at the Royal and Ancient Course in heaven, praise God for giving you this person as an influence.

Continue developing a pattern of writing in your journal a few times each week. Don't let the end of the study be the end of this practice; seek to make it part of your normal spiritual growth.

> We all need an old pro and we can all be an old pro.

JOURNAL

Solid Shots

_____

_____

_____

_____

_____

_____

_____

Mulligans

_____

_____

_____

_____

_____

_____

_____

LEADER'S GUIDE
How to Lead a Small Group
Discussion of *The Mulligan*

Creating a safe environment that fosters great discussions is critical to the success of a good small group experience. The key is preparation. This leader's guide contains suggestions that will help your group gain from the insights of each participant, promote openness, and foster discussion.

BEFORE THE FIRST MEETING:

1. Pray for each person that has been invited.
2. Plan ahead for a location that provides a quiet environment with no outside distractions.
3. Make sure that there is adequate lighting as well as enough seating for each group member. In other words, make it comfortable.
4. Make sure that each person who has been invited has had an opportunity to read *The Mulligan* book beforehand. Be prepared to distribute a copy of this participant's guide to each person at the first session, if not before. Make sure each participant understands what the discussion group is all about and what will happen in the group time together.
5. Limit the group to a maximum of six to eight people. Ideally, your group would contain a foursome or two with whom you have played golf before.
6. If possible, plan on a round of golf either before or after each session.
7. Clearly define the time limit for each meeting. We suggest that the actual meeting time be limited to no more than one hour. Be punctual when beginning and ending each meeting.

AT EACH MEETING:

1. Make sure that everyone in the group has had an opportunity to meet each other at the start of session one. Also, make sure that

everyone is comfortable. Providing coffee, tea, or soda can be very helpful.

2. Each of the six sessions of *The Mulligan* video study follows a basic, easy-to-follow outline (the participant's guide provides instructions throughout each session to move everyone along):

I. Welcome/Introduction

Welcome each group member and pray if you would like. Either read or summarize the session introduction from the participant's guide, or skip directly to the first video segment.

II. Video Segment (Part One) — Introduction, Golf Story, and Golf Tip

Play the first portion of the session video.

III. Talk About It

Take a couple minutes to answer the theme-related icebreaker questions provided in the participant's guide.

IV. Video Segment (Part Two) — Main Session with Wally/ Closing Challenge with Ken

Play the second portion of the session video. Encourage group members to take notes in the space provided in the participant's guide.

V. Video Discussion

Discuss as many questions from this section of the participant's guide as time permits. Bring along extra Bibles for those who may volunteer to read the Scripture passages or want to follow along.

VI. "Between Sessions" Instructions and Closing Prayer

Point out the "Between Sessions" activities in the participant's guide and encourage group members to complete them before your next meeting. Then wrap up with prayer, using any of the suggestions offered in the participant's guide.

PROMOTING A HEALTHY DISCUSSION:

1. If your group includes people from different faiths or from no faith at all, seek to prevent a defensive tone by promoting an open, supportive atmosphere. Be sensitive and make them feel comfortable and accepted.

2. Avoid using religious language or technical theological words or clichés that are unclear to group members. Avoid mentioning denominations or other faiths by name.
3. Avoid stifling discussion with pat answers. Encourage discussion by asking the opinions of others.
4. Critique ideas without criticizing the people who express those ideas.
5. Maintain good eye contact with each participant.
6. Develop good listening habits. Be an empathetic, understanding, active listener to each participant. Listen for expression of interests in personal backgrounds, felt needs, and previous religious experiences, without pressure or condescension.
7. Make people feel they can say anything and still be accepted and appreciated.
8. When making statements or casual comments during the discussion, be sure to show openness to other participants' perspectives while promoting continued discussion.
9. Use questions to promote discussion. Ask for clarification. Answer objections with questions. Ask probing, provocative, challenging questions.
10. Ask "feeling" questions rather than "factual" questions.

STIMULATING A GOOD DISCUSSION:

1. When you want another person to say more:
   - *"I'm just wondering, have you ever considered this ...?"*
   - *"Can I give you another option?"*
   - *"How would you respond to ...?"*

2. When you agree:
   - *"Thanks for sharing."*
   - *"That's an excellent observation."*
   - *"I appreciate your perspective."*

3. When you want to express your disagreement:
   - *"What you are saying raises some red flags in my mind."*
   - *"My perception on this issue is a little different; may I share it with you?"*

- *"Correct me if I am wrong, but I see a conflict between _____ and _____."*

4. When you want to stimulate discussion from others in the group:
   - *"I would be interested in _____'s reaction to that."*
   - *"How does what you are saying relate to his comment?"*
   - *"What do some of the rest of you think about what he just said?"*

ENDING A GOOD DISCUSSION:

1. Again, be punctual. End the meeting on time whether you have finished the discussion or not.
2. Encourage the participants to continue discussing issues with each other after the group discussion time.
3. Again, be sensitive to those who participated in the discussion. Depending on the participants, decide ahead of time whether to end the discussion time in prayer or not. If you do end the discussion time in prayer, it should be the leader who prays if no one else is comfortable in doing so. Keep it simple and short.
4. Provide a brief verbal summary of the discussion.
5. Invite the participants to the next session, giving them the time and location.

The Mulligan

A Parable of Second Chances

*Ken Blanchard and Wally Armstrong
with Kevin Harney*

In this hardcover book endorsed by golf legend Jack Nicklaus and written in the appealing parable style of other bestselling books such as *Who Moved My Cheese?*; *Gungo Ho!*; and *Whale Done!*; golf pro Wally Armstrong and author Ken Blanchard walk you through time-tested steps for improving your golf game and your life.

Told through the eyes of Paul McAllister, the Ivy League–educated founder of a multimillion dollar business, this inspiring story about relationships, forgiveness, and priorities is the shot of grace you've been looking for.

Golf's gracious do-over, a mulligan is the beginning of Paul's own second chance. Guided by the wisdom and advice of an old pro, Paul learns about priorities, self-confidence, and playing a good game both on and off the course.

If you ever thought it would be great to do some things over in life— to get a second chance—in the grip of golf pro Wally Armstrong and Ken Blanchard, author of the bestselling *The One Minute Manager*, *The Mulligan* becomes a life-changing principle.

Available in stores and online!

Share Your Thoughts

With the Author: Your comments will be forwarded to the author when you send them to *zauthor@zondervan.com*.

With Zondervan: Submit your review of this book by writing to *zreview@zondervan.com*.

Free Online Resources at
www.zondervan.com

Zondervan AuthorTracker: Be notified whenever your favorite authors publish new books, go on tour, or post an update about what's happening in their lives at www.zondervan.com/authortracker.

Daily Bible Verses and Devotions: Enrich your life with daily Bible verses or devotions that help you start every morning focused on God. Visit www.zondervan.com/newsletters.

Free Email Publications: Sign up for newsletters on Christian living, academic resources, church ministry, fiction, children's resources, and more. Visit www.zondervan.com/newsletters.

Zondervan Bible Search: Find and compare Bible passages in a variety of translations at www.zondervanbiblesearch.com.

Other Benefits: Register yourself to receive online benefits like coupons and special offers, or to participate in research.